Specific Skill Series

Getting the Main Idea

Richard A. Boning

Fifth Edition

SRA/McGraw-Hill
Columbus, Ohio

Cover, Back Cover, Jonathan Scott/Masterfile

SRA/McGraw-Hill

A Division of The McGraw·Hill Companies

Printed in the United States of America.

Send all inquiries to:
    SRA/McGraw-Hill
    8787 Orion Place
    Columbus, OH 43240-4027

ISBN 0-02-687976-X

   10 WAL 05

PURPOSE:

GETTING THE MAIN IDEA is designed to assist pupils in grasping the central thought of a short passage. This skill is not only one of the most important of all major skills, but one which must be developed from the earliest stages.

FOR WHOM:

The skill of GETTING THE MAIN IDEA is developed through a series of books spanning ten levels (Picture, Preparatory, A, B, C, D, E, F, G, H). The Picture Level is for pupils who have not acquired a basic sight vocabulary. The Preparatory Level is for pupils who have a basic sight vocabulary but are not yet ready for the first-grade-level book. Books A through H are appropriate for pupils who can read on levels one through eight, respectively. **The use of the *Specific Skill Series Placement Test* is recommended to determine the appropriate level.**

THE NEW EDITION:

The fifth edition of the *Specific Skill Series* maintains the quality and focus that has distinguished this program for more than 25 years. A key element central to the program's success has been the unique nature of the reading selections. Nonfiction pieces about current topics have been designed to stimulate the interest of students, motivating them to use the comprehension strategies they have learned to further their reading. To keep this important aspect of the program intact, a percentage of the reading selections have been replaced in order to ensure the continued relevance of the subject material.

In addition, a significant percentage of the artwork in the program has been replaced to give the books a contemporary look. The cover photographs are designed to appeal to readers of all ages.

SESSIONS:

Short practice sessions are the most effective. It is desirable to have a practice session every day or every other day, using a few units each session.

SCORING:

Pupils should record their answers on the reproducible worksheets. The worksheets make scoring easier and provide uniform records of the pupils' work. Using worksheets also avoids consuming exercise books.

To the Teacher

It is important for pupils to know how well they are doing. For this reason, units should be scored as soon as they have been completed. Then a discussion can be held in which pupils justify their choices. (The Integrated Language Activities, many of which are open-ended, do not lend themselves to an objective score; thus there are no answer keys for these pages.)

GENERAL INFORMATION ON *GETTING THE MAIN IDEA:*

There are several ways by which teachers can help pupils identify main ideas.

A. **Topic Words:** Pupils tell in a word or two the topic of the paragraph.

B. **Key Question Words:** Pupils learn that questions can begin with special words: *Why, Where, When, How,* and *What.*

C. **Place Clues:** Pupils become aware of paragraph structure. They learn that the main idea is often stated in the first or last sentence.

D. **Space Clues:** Pupils learn that the central thought of a paragraph is not limited to a single sentence, even though it may be stated in one sentence.

E. **Turnabout Clues:** If the main idea is stated in one sentence, pupils learn to change that sentence into a question and see if the whole paragraph answers it.

F. **General and Specific Ideas:** Pupils understand that some words are more general or inclusive than others. Pupils compare sentences to determine which are more inclusive and which are supporting sentences.

SUGGESTED STEPS:

1. Pupils read the passage. (On the Picture Level, they look at the picture.)
2. After reading each passage (or looking at the picture), the readers select its main idea. The choices are on the opposite page (or below the picture/passage, at the Picture, Preparatory, and A levels).

Additional information on using GETTING THE MAIN IDEA with pupils will be found in the **Specific Skill Series Teacher's Manual**.

RELATED MATERIALS:

Specific Skill Series Placement Tests, which enable the teacher to place pupils at their appropriate levels in each skill, are available for the Elementary (Pre-1–6) and Midway (4–8) grade levels.

About This Book

A picture, a paragraph, or a story is about something. It has a topic, or subject. The **main idea** tells about the subject. The main idea of a paragraph is the most important idea the writer is trying to state. You can think of a main idea as being like a tree. The tree has many parts—a trunk, roots, leaves, branches. All these parts together add up to make the whole tree. In the same way, the **details** in a paragraph add up to tell about the main idea.

Sometimes, the main idea is stated in a sentence. This is often the first or last sentence in a paragraph. In the following paragraph, the main idea is stated in the first sentence. The other sentences in the paragraph are details. They tell more about the main idea.

> The bloodhound's keen sense of smell can be very useful to people. Bloodhounds are better at tracking people than any other dog. If a person is lost, a trained bloodhound may be given a piece of that person's clothing to sniff. The bloodhound can often find the person by following the scent left by the person's feet, even if the track is several hours old.

Sometimes, there is no main idea sentence. Then you need to think about the information in all of the sentences and figure out what the main idea is. Read this paragraph. Ask yourself, "What is the paragraph mainly about?"

> Each honeybee colony has one queen bee. The queen bee is the only bee that lays eggs. Worker bees are other female bees. They do all of the chores in the colony. They gather food, build the hive, and care for the young. The colony also include male bees that do no work. These are called drones.

This sentence tells the main idea:

> A honeybee colony includes three types of bees: a queen, worker bees, and drones.

In this book, you will read paragraphs. Then you will decide what each paragraph is mainly about. You will use the information in the paragraph to figure out the main idea.

1. Compared with the fourteen-thousand-foot peaks of the Rockies, Mt. Washington in New Hampshire may seem relatively small at 6,288 feet high. However, the top of Mt. Washington has unbelievably treacherous weather. In moments the weather can change from a sunny to a stormy day—often with fierce gales. No wonder the building on this mountaintop is chained to the ground!

2. Many fighters for women's equality say it's about time the United States put a woman's portrait on some of its paper money. Few people know, however, that two women have already achieved that honor, a century ago. Martha Washington's face graced a one-dollar bill and Pocahontas' picture appeared on a twenty-dollar bank note.

3. Trees use and give off a surprising amount of water. The water is taken in by the roots and released by the leaves. It has been estimated that eighty gallons of water a day may evaporate from the average tree. A white oak tree will give off 150 gallons of moisture in a single day during hot weather. A large oak tree will give off 28,000 gallons of water during one growing season!

4. The North Pole is not the world's coldest region. Northeastern Siberia, over one thousand miles south of the North Pole, is the coldest place on earth. Temperatures as low as eighty degrees below zero Fahrenheit (-62.2 Celsius) have often been recorded. Oddly enough, you would seldom catch a cold in the world's coldest region. Most germs cannot live in such extreme cold!

5. The mystery of how salmon can find their way back to their home rivers is solved. A salmon navigates by sun and stars when traveling in the ocean. When the salmon nears the general area of the river in which it was born, it uses its nose. The salmon can remember the smell of the home river that it left as a baby.

1. The paragraph tells mainly—

   (A) why people climb to the top of Mt. Washington
   (B) why Mt. Washington is smaller than the Rockies
   (C) why the weather can change so fast at the top of Mt. Washington
   (D) why the top of Mt. Washington is treacherous

2. The paragraph tells mainly—

   (A) why women should be pictured on paper money
   (B) when women's portraits were printed on paper money
   (C) how people fight for equality
   (D) why women are no longer pictured on paper money

3. The paragraph tells mainly—

   (A) how much water trees give off
   (B) how trees give off water
   (C) what trees give off the least water
   (D) how trees take in water

4. The paragraph tells mainly—

   (A) how cold it gets
   (B) why people don't catch cold
   (C) what the coldest region is like
   (D) what the North Pole is like

5. The paragraph tells mainly—

   (A) what a mystery is
   (B) how far salmon travel
   (C) what salmon remember
   (D) how salmon find their way home

1.   In eighteenth-century England, unusually severe punishments were often given out for minor crimes. The laws listed over two hundred kinds of crimes punishable by death. A person could be hanged for stealing rabbits, being too friendly with gypsies, or cutting down a tree that stood on public land.

2.   Mark Twain once wrote a story about a frog-jumping contest in Calaveras County, California. In this story, one frog's owner puts buckshot into another frog's mouth. The poor frog is so heavy, it can't jump at all. Because that story became so popular, people in Calaveras County today hold a Jumping Frog Jubilee every year.

3.   Broken bones are referred to as either compound or simple fractures. What is the difference? Many people believe that a simple fracture means a single break and a compound fracture means multiple breaks. This is not true. A simple fracture is one in which the broken bone does not pierce the skin. A compound fracture is one in which the fracture is exposed through a wound in the skin.

4.   A dog was transported by a roundabout route to a point about thirty blocks from home. When the animal was released, it explored a little. After stopping to play with other dogs, it reached its home by an indirect route that covered some five miles and took about seventy minutes. When the experiment was repeated, it reached home in about half the time.

5.   Every February, Quebec City has a winter carnival. There are parades, street dances, costume balls, and sports events. People carve attractive monuments from ice and snow. The ice sculptures, narrow zigzagging streets, horse-drawn sleighs, and colored streetlights add a picture-book setting to two weeks of fun in the French-speaking Canadian city.

UNIT 2

1. The paragraph tells mainly—

    (A) what the punishment for stealing rabbits was
    (B) what life in old England was like
    (C) how eighteenth-century England dealt with small crimes
    (D) how the eighteenth-century English caught criminals

2. The paragraph tells mainly—

    (A) why Mark Twain's stories became so popular
    (B) why a frog was named Daniel Webster
    (C) where Mark Twain wrote his story about a frog-jumping contest
    (D) why a frog-jumping contest is held in Calaveras County

3. The paragraph tells mainly—

    (A) what causes fractures
    (B) how compound and simple fractures differ
    (C) what a compound fracture is
    (D) where fractures occur

4. The paragraph tells mainly—

    (A) what experiment was made with a dog
    (B) how far the dog traveled
    (C) why the dog stopped to play on its way home
    (D) how fast the dog ran

5. The paragraph tells mainly—

    (A) why Quebec City has a winter carnival
    (B) how the snow helps
    (C) what the ice and snow monuments look like
    (D) what the winter carnival in Quebec City is like

1.   Rudy Salazar, an auto mechanic in Concord, California, has been blind since birth. He was always interested in cars and their engines, which he studied in high school, junior college, and in special courses given by the State Rehabilitation Program. He learned to "feel" what he was doing when he reached under the hood. By listening to the engine's sound, Rudy detects many mechanical problems.

---

2.   Almost two hundred years ago a famous French balloonist came to Philadelphia to popularize balloon flights in the United States. A launching on January 9, 1793, marked the first aerial voyage in North America and was witnessed by a crowd of fifty thousand people. The balloon passed over the Delaware River and landed near Woodbury, New Jersey.

---

3.   The great Tillamook fire took place in August of 1933. This fire turned 270,000 acres of Oregon forests into ashes, amounting to a loss of almost twelve billion board feet of lumber. Twelve billion board feet is a staggering quantity. It is as much as all the timber cut in all the forests of the United States in the year before the disastrous Tillamook fire occurred.

---

4.   Earthquakes sometimes follow a pattern of foreshocks, main shocks, and aftershocks. Foreshocks may be very strong, almost major earthquakes, or very feeble and hardly felt. The main shock, of course, is larger than the rest. Aftershocks, though smaller than the main shock, can do extensive damage to buildings weakened by earlier shaking. They may continue on and off for days or even years.

---

5.   What was the greatest robbery in history? In 1945, just after Germany surrendered in World War II, robbers stole the German national gold reserves. They stole seven hundred gold bars and boxes of gems and currency. The robbery was committed while this treasure was being transferred to a new location. The value of the loot was estimated at well over $3.75 billion. The booty was never recovered, and the robbers were never identified.

1. The paragraph tells mainly—

    (A) when Rudy Salazar lost his sight

    (B) why Salazar became interested in cars and engines

    (C) how a blind man became a successful auto mechanic

    (D) where Rudy Salazar learned about cars and engines

---

2. The paragraph tells mainly—

    (A) why people like balloons

    (B) how far the French balloon went from Philadelphia in 1793

    (C) what the first balloon trip in North America was like

    (D) why the French balloonist was famous

---

3. The paragraph tells mainly—

    (A) where Tillamook is

    (B) how destructive the Tillamook fire was

    (C) what happened in 1933

    (D) how the Tillamook fire started

---

4. The paragraph tells mainly—

    (A) what foreshocks are

    (B) how long aftershocks last

    (C) what the pattern of earthquakes is

    (D) how all earthquakes damage buildings

---

5. The paragraph tells mainly—

    (A) who the robbers of the gold reserves were

    (B) what was recovered

    (C) how the biggest robbery occurred

    (D) what the value of the loot was

1.   Why does a mustang buck so wildly when a saddle or rider is on its back for the first time? Mustangs have the blood of wild horses. Their ancestors roamed the plains, hunted by wolves and mountain lions. They had a built-in terror of being attacked and killed by fang and claw. Instinctively they became all fear and fire when something leaped on their backs.

2.   The lamprey is a water animal that resembles an eel. Its skin is smooth and shiny, but dull in color. Its mouth is round. The lamprey attaches its ugly mouth to the body of a fish and sucks all its victim's blood. Thus this eellike creature destroys trout and other fish in the Great Lakes and elsewhere.

3.   In colonial days, garments were stiffened with starch. Starch-making was an involved process. Potatoes were grated into tubs of water through tin sheets pierced by nails. The skins floated to the surface and were discarded, while the starch sank to the bottom of the tub. After being removed, the starch slowly dried into a pure white cake, which was then crumbled into powder.

4.   It happened just about a century ago, but people still talk about the blizzard of 1888. It began on March 11. In four days four feet of snow fell in New York and New England. Winds up to eighty miles an hour piled the snow in huge drifts. Doorways were buried. People climbed in and out of their second-floor windows. As people said later, "Who could forget it?"

5.   The state of Delaware has several nicknames. Some call it the "Blue Hen State" because of the fighting record of its Revolutionary War troops, who were compared to the game chickens carried by some of the soldiers. Another favorite nickname is "The First State." Delaware was the first of the thirteen original colonies to accept the Constitution in 1787.

1. The paragraph tells mainly—

   (A) what the mustangs' ancestors did
   (B) what animals killed mustangs
   (C) what makes mustangs buck wildly
   (D) why horses are difficult to train

2. The paragraph tells mainly—

   (A) why fish die
   (B) what lampreys do
   (C) what the lamprey's mouth is like
   (D) what the lamprey's skin is like

3. The paragraph tells mainly—

   (A) why garments were starched in colonial days
   (B) how starch pudding is made
   (C) how the colonists made starch
   (D) how the colonists used potatoes

4. The paragraph tells mainly—

   (A) how much snow fell
   (B) what causes blizzards
   (C) what effect the wind had
   (D) what the blizzard was like

5. The paragraph tells mainly—

   (A) how Delaware got its real name
   (B) why some chickens were blue
   (C) why Delaware was the first to accept the Constitution
   (D) how Delaware got its nicknames

1. For a century, people had searched for dinosaur eggs without success. In 1923 an American expedition trekked into the Gobi Desert. There, by chance, the scientists made a historical discovery—a nest of thirteen eggs of the hornless Protoceratops. The oval, seven-inch eggs had been preserved for centuries by drifting sand. Since that time dinosaur eggs have been discovered at a number of places.

2. The ancient Mexicans found many uses for the maguey plant. It provided paper, thread, needles, pins, soap, medicine, food, and drink. After the food was taken from the heart of the plant, the center filled up with juice called honey water. The leaves could be used as cleaning pads, for thatched roofs, and for siding on houses. Maguey plants became a fence when planted closely together.

3. There is an old expression, "Rome wasn't built in a day." This saying means that people cannot expect to accomplish something very worthwhile in just a short time. The larger the task, the greater the time needed to accomplish it. This expression tells us to be patient as we try to reach our goals.

4. Giant snowslides called avalanches travel at different rates of speed. The airborne powder avalanche—where the dry, loose snow lifts off the ground and swirls through the air—usually travels about one hundred miles per hour. Dry snow avalanches travel about twenty-five miles per hour. Wet snow avalanches travel about fifteen miles per hour.

5. For years the United States Navy has used sealed bottles to help study the course and speed of ocean currents. Bottles carrying printed letters in various languages are set afloat. Finders are asked to write the time and place of discovery and return this information, which is valuable in preparing charts of ocean currents.

1. The paragraph tells mainly—

   (A) why people searched for dinosaur eggs
   (B) how big dinosaur eggs are
   (C) how the American expedition ended
   (D) why dinosaur eggs are scarce

2. The paragraph tells mainly—

   (A) how maguey leaves were used for building homes
   (B) what drink was produced from the maguey plant
   (C) what the maguey plant looked like
   (D) how ancient Mexicans used the maguey plant

3. The paragraph tells mainly—

   (A) how Rome was constructed
   (B) what an old expression means
   (C) how long it took to build Rome
   (D) what people expect

4. The paragraph tells mainly—

   (A) how to avoid an avalanche
   (B) why airborne avalanches travel so fast
   (C) how fast avalanches travel
   (D) why some avalanches travel slowly

5. The paragraph tells mainly—

   (A) how charts of ocean currents help the Navy
   (B) why people use bottles
   (C) how the Navy studies ocean currents
   (D) what to do with sealed bottles

UNIT 6

1.   Parachutes were invented long before the first airplane flight, but the idea of an airplane itself descending in a parachute certainly is new. A recent invention permits a plane in trouble to throw out a parachute that will bring the craft safely back to earth. The inventors hope that large airlines will accept their invention. It is part of the continuing war on air tragedies.

2.   On October 8, 1871, a terrible fire destroyed much forest land around Green Bay, Wisconsin. More than 1,200 people were killed. But the fire was largely unnoticed because it happened on the same day as the great Chicago fire, which got all the attention.

3.   Throughout most of the towns and cities of Holland, musicians can be seen playing violins and accordions. Crowds gather on street corners to hear some toe-tapping tunes. Huge organs mounted on brightly painted wagons are pushed from corner to corner. Sometimes these wagons are horse-drawn. These handcranked barrel organs fill city streets with songs that set people's feet dancing.

4.   To get sled dogs moving, the driver tells them to "mush." What does this word mean? Early French Canadians got sled dogs into action by shouting, "Marchons!" This French word means "Let us march." Later, English sled drivers tried to use the same word, but they were unable to pronounce it. They commanded their dogs to "mushon"—then simply to "mush."

5.   It was in Boston that the spark of liberty was kindled by America's colonial patriots. The first clash between British troops and colonists took place there. Not far away, in Lexington and Concord, the first battles of the Revolution were fought. The Freedom Trail runs through the center of Boston. The city's other historical sights include the Old North Church, the Revere house, and Faneuil Hall.

16

1. The paragraph tells mainly—

    (A) when the first parachute was invented
    (B) how airplanes came down
    (C) what the new parachute does
    (D) why there is a war against air tragedies

2. The paragraph tells mainly—

    (A) about the forests of Green Bay
    (B) about the Wisconsin forest fire
    (C) why Chicago is more important than Green Bay
    (D) about the death toll of the Wisconsin fire

3. The paragraph tells mainly—

    (A) why Hollanders like the violin
    (B) how much Hollanders like music
    (C) why people like music
    (D) what happens in city streets

4. The paragraph tells mainly—

    (A) how difficult it is to speak French
    (B) why dogs understand different languages
    (C) how the command to "mush" originated
    (D) who first used sled dogs

5. The paragraph tells mainly—

    (A) who America's colonial patriots were
    (B) where the Revolution took place
    (C) what happened at Lexington and Concord
    (D) what makes Boston so historic

A. Exercising Your Skill

In Unit 5 you learned about the maguey plant. Now consider another plant that is useful to people: the dandelion.

Early European settlers in America brought the dandelion with them for food and medicine. They boiled the white, fleshy root in water and ate it as a vegetable. They ground the roots, cooked them, and used them in preparing a coffee-like drink. The young tender leaves of the plant were used in salads or eaten like spinach. As a medicine, the plant was once the official cure for sicknesses that came on the settlers in the winter. Though many people today consider dandelions a nuisance, they have had their uses.

Write a title that sums up the main idea of the paragraph.

_____

Some people consider the dandelion a hardy plant. Others think of it only as a pesty weed. Whether you like the dandelion or not, you must agree that it is an amazing plant. A single plant in a huge field can multiply so quickly that in a few years the whole field will be covered in dandelions, and they are hard to get rid of. You can dig up a dandelion plant, roots and all. But you had better not toss it into a corner of the yard. If you do that, the dandelion will still produce seeds. The seeds will be carried through the air and produce many more plants.

Write a title that sums up the main idea of the paragraph.

_____

B. Expanding Your Skill

Go back to each paragraph to find the sentence that best states its main idea. Remember, the main idea sentence will not always be the first sentence in the paragraph. Write the main idea sentences on your paper.

Paragraph One _____

Paragraph Two _____

C. Exploring Language

Read the paragraph to identify the main idea sentence. Then, on your paper, write the main idea sentence and two supporting sentences.

Every plant has two names. One, such as *dandelion*, is its common name. The other, such as *taraxacum officinale*, is the Latin name (for the dandelion). There may be many plants that carry the same common name, but each plant has only one Latin name. However, Latin is a dead language. Having an international code does away with any possible confusion in talking about a particular plant. For example, the flower we commonly call the marigold is really the French or African marigold. There is also a swamp, or marsh, marigold, which is quite a different kind of flower. Marigolds are quite beautiful.

Main Idea Sentence: _____

Supporting Sentence: _____

Supporting Sentence: _____

D. Expressing Yourself

Choose one of these activities.

1. Choose one other wild plant. Prepare a written list of ways in which this plant is useful to people. Some possible choices of wild plants are—

    cattail, maple, mint, watercress

2. Find some recipes that use wild plants. Share the recipes with your classmates. If possible, work with an adult to make one of the dishes.

3. Use a library book on plant identification to find out the common names for these wild plants.

    Acer saccharum _____

    Typha latifolia _____

    Mentha piperita _____

    Nasturtium officinale _____

1. Sometimes snow that hasn't been white has fallen. Snowfalls have been blue, green, red, and even black! Snowflakes are tiny frozen crystals that have gathered around something in the atmosphere, usually a drop of water. When enough crystals come together, their weight makes them fall to the ground. If snowflakes form around colored dust in the atmosphere, the snow will be the color of the dust.

2. Tapioca comes from the root of the cassava plant, which is highly poisonous when uncooked. The food was discovered when a Spanish explorer was lost in the jungles of Brazil. Preferring a quick death to slow starvation, the explorer cooked cassava roots in water and drank the mixture. Surprisingly, the explorer not only survived but also found the food delicious!

3. The charm and originality of Mexican handicrafts is recognized the world over. Nearly every village and town specializes in some fine handicraft. Taxco, for example, is famous for jewelry. Guadalajara is known for its hand-blown glass. The crafts workers of Pueblo produce unique pottery. For many hundreds of years, Mexicans have been making beautiful things with their hands.

4. In 1913, airplanes were involved in aerial combat for the first time. This battle differed from modern aerial warfare. It involved two American pilots. Fighting on opposite sides during a Mexican revolution, they met in the sky over Noco, Mexico, and exchanged pistol shots. Neither of the pilots was killed or wounded.

5. In the early 1800s, a southern colonel named W.H. Jackson liked to sit under a particular oak tree. He didn't want the tree to be destroyed if someone else owned the property after he died. So all the land within eight feet of the trunk was deeded to the tree in 1820. Although the tree was destroyed by a storm in 1942, its direct descendant is still growing today.

1.   The paragraph tells mainly—

   (A) what snow crystals are
   (B) how dust can change snowflakes
   (C) how snowflakes are formed
   (D) why snowflakes are sometimes colorful

---

2.   The paragraph tells mainly—

   (A) who discovered tapioca
   (B) how. tapioca was discovered
   (C) how to cook tapioca
   (D) what plant tapioca comes from

---

3.   The paragraph tells mainly—

   (A) who makes pottery
   (B) why Mexicans make beautiful things
   (C) how fast Mexicans work
   (D) what some famous Mexican handicrafts are

---

4.   The paragraph tells mainly—

   (A) what happened in 1913
   (B) what happened to two pilots
   (C) what the first aerial battle was like
   (D) what warfare was like long ago

---

5.   The paragraph tells mainly—

   (A) what kind of tree Colonel Jackson liked
   (B) how and when the oak tree was destroyed
   (C) how Colonel Jackson protected his favorite oak tree
   (D) where the surviving oak tree is located

1.   The practice of wearing rings is a very ancient one. Over time, people in many lands have decorated their bodies by wearing rings on their fingers, ears, lips, necks, noses, ankles, and wrists. Some even wore rings on their toes. In some cultures, a married woman wore a ring on the big toe of her left foot; a man might put rings on his second and third toes as well.

2.   The frankfurter, named for the city of Frankfurt in Germany, is easily the most popular sausage in the world. Frankfurters, popularly known as "hot dogs," are sold almost everywhere in the United States. They are consumed in great numbers at sporting events and amusement places. People from foreign countries often think hot dogs are one of the characteristics of American life.

3.   Many ancient coins are not as valuable as people tend to think they are. In the early days, the threat of a foreign invasion was common. People buried the family wealth, hoping to uncover it later when the threat was past. In many cases these people were killed or taken away as prisoners. Their coins are continually being uncovered by chance today and can be purchased for a modest price.

4.   The Trans-Canadian Highway is the first ocean-to-ocean highway in Canada and the longest paved road in the world. After twelve years of work, the 4,859-mile highway was completed in September of 1962. The Trans-Canadian Highway makes it possible, for the first time, for a person to drive from coast to coast and remain within Canada for the entire trip.

5.   The experts are not always right. They advised the big mining companies to pass up the Cripple Creek region. They claimed that there was no gold there. It was left up to local prospectors to uncover the incredible wealth of Cripple Creek. More than $400 million worth of ore was found in this area that experts ignored.

1. The paragraph tells mainly—

    (A) why some people wore rings on their toes
    (B) what kinds of rings were the most popular
    (C) when the practice of wearing rings first began
    (D) how people in many lands have worn rings

2. The paragraph tells mainly—

    (A) why hot dogs are popular
    (B) how popular hot dogs are
    (C) what foreign people think of hot dogs
    (D) how hot dogs and frankfurters differ

3. The paragraph tells mainly—

    (A) what happened during invasions
    (B) why there are so few ancient coins today
    (C) why many ancient coins are inexpensive
    (D) why people were taken prisoners

4. The paragraph tells mainly—

    (A) what the Trans-Canadian Highway is like
    (B) how the Trans-Canadian Highway helps
    (C) why the Trans-Canadian Highway was built
    (D) where the longest road is

5. The paragraph tells mainly—

    (A) what experts thought about Cripple Creek
    (B) when the Cripple Creek gold was found
    (C) how much the ore was worth
    (D) how big mining companies operated

1. Native peoples were astonishing astronomers. They had no tools—no telescopes, no computers, not even any eyeglasses to improve their eyesight. Yet the Maya people of Central America and the Yucatan made accurate observations of the skies and made predictions about the movements of Venus. These predictions rival our computer predictions today.

2. Ann Fitzpatrick makes the sweetest statues. She builds them out of gumdrops. She learned to do this while she was recovering from a skiing accident. She first makes a paste of sugar, then shapes it and sticks gumdrops onto it. She makes castles, dolls, toy-size cars, and even life-size humans. You probably wouldn't eat one of Ann Fitzpatrick's statues, however. They look too good—and may cost more than $700.

3. The governor of New York signed a bill in 1933 that outlawed any dance lasting longer than eight hours. The law was aimed at dance marathons. After each hour of dancing in the marathons, couples were allowed fifteen minutes to rest or eat. In order to win prizes, couples would often dance their way to exhaustion. The law stepped in to stop the dangerous fad.

4. During the early days of our country, most people ate corn twice a day, day after day, year after year, all their lives. Some people ate corn three times a day. Often it was mixed with water or milk. Then it was boiled for hours, with much stirring, till it formed a rather solid pudding. This was called hasty pudding.

5. One of the greatest avalanche disasters in the history of the United States occurred in 1910 at Wellington, Washington. Three trains were hurled into a canyon by a single snowslide. More than a hundred people were killed. One of the greatest avalanche disasters in the world occurred during World War I. In a period of twenty-four hours, five thousand Austrian and Italian soldiers were buried alive by an avalanche in the Alps.

1. The paragraph tells mainly—

   (A) about the movements of Venus

   (B) about the skill of the Maya astronomers

   (C) why the Maya had such poor eyesight

   (D) where in Central America the Maya lived

2. The paragraph tells mainly—

   (A) how Ann Fitzpatrick was injured

   (B) where Ann Fitzpatrick lives

   (C) why Ann Fitzpatrick uses gumdrops for her statues

   (D) what unusual skill Ann Fitzpatrick has

3. The paragraph tells mainly—

   (A) how long dance marathons lasted

   (B) why the law had to stop marathon dances

   (C) how couples won prizes for dancing

   (D) when the dance marathon was a fad

4. The paragraph tells mainly—

   (A) why people raise corn

   (B) how delicious hasty pudding is

   (C) how much corn people ate long ago

   (D) why people like the taste of corn so much

5. The paragraph tells mainly—

   (A) where avalanches have occurred

   (B) how destructive avalanches can be

   (C) what the most destructive avalanches were

   (D) how powerful avalanches can be

UNIT 10

1.   Japanese fishers long ago figured out how nature could help them catch fish. The fishers have trained big birds, called cormorants, to do most of their work. Fishing from boats at night, the Japanese hang fires in baskets over the sides of their boats. Fish are attracted by the fire. The cormorants, on leashes, grab the fish, and the fishers grab the fish from the birds.

2.   The Johnstown flood was the worst in United States history. On the afternoon of May 31, 1889, heavy rains caused a dam to break fifteen miles above Johnstown, Pennsylvania. A wall of water about thirty feet high and weighing millions of tons raced down the valley, sweeping everything with it — houses, trees, locomotives, animals, telegraph poles, and over two thousand people!

3.   In August of 1873 the first hydrogen-filled balloon was launched in Paris. It landed near a little village fifteen miles away. The peasants were terrified. They thought it was a monster from another world. One fired a shot into it, allowing the hydrogen to escape. Others tore the balloon to shreds with their pitchforks.

4.   The Carlsbad Caverns of New Mexico contain the largest known single open space below the surface of the earth. This giant room is 4,270 feet long, 656 feet wide, and 328 feet high. A twenty-eight-story skyscraper could fit inside. To this day, parts of this cavern remain unexplored, even though many years have passed since it was first entered.

5.   Many people believe that sleigh bells were merely ornamental. This is not so. Bells were once a necessary part of winter traffic. In the days when there were no sidewalks, people walked on the roads. Sleighs drawn through the snow were fast and silent. Moreover, sound was partly muffled by earmuffs. Sleighs not equipped with bells were a genuine danger to those walking in traffic.

1. The paragraph tells mainly—

   (A) what kind of fish the Japanese catch
   (B) where the Japanese catch fish
   (C) how the Japanese catch fish
   (D) why the Japanese catch fish

---

2. The paragraph tells mainly—

   (A) what the cause of the Johnstown flood was
   (B) how fast the Johnstown flood destroyed the city
   (C) how destructive the Johnstown flood was
   (D) what people thought about the flood

---

3. The paragraph tells mainly—

   (A) what the first hydrogen-filled-balloon flight proved
   (B) what hydrogen is
   (C) what happened to the first hydrogen-filled balloon
   (D) why the first balloon was filled with hydrogen

---

4. The paragraph tells mainly—

   (A) why people explore the Carlsbad Caverns
   (B) who discovered the largest cave
   (C) what the height of the room is
   (D) how large one room in the Carlsbad Caverns is

---

5. The paragraph tells mainly—

   (A) why people once walked on the road
   (B) how fast sleighs were
   (C) why sleighs had bells
   (D) why there were accidents

1.   A cat is often referred to today as a "tabby." The name began long ago in the Arab city of Baghdad. The famous silk bazaar of Baghdad was called "Attabi," the name for a special silk fabric with a rippled pattern resembling the coats of certain cats. It was easy for buyers to see the resemblance.

---

2.   Every year about the third week of September there is a festival in Lunenberg, Nova Scotia. This old shipbuilding community, home of the racing champion of the Atlantic, the famous *Bluenose*, is also the home of many fishers and lobster catchers. Rowboat races and fish-filleting contests are just a few of the reminders of the seafaring tradition of Lunenberg.

---

3.   Did you ever hear of a "silent sound"? There is such a thing. Silent sounds are the sounds that we can't hear with our ears. When there are very few vibrations per second, we can't hear any sound. When there are more than twenty-thousand vibrations per second, we also can't hear. This is the world of ultrasonics, the strange world of "silent sound."

---

4.   Jet fighters can "shoot themselves down"—by accident, of course. Say a plane is flying nine hundred miles per hour. It fires a shell which leaves the gun at two thousand miles per hour. The shell soon slows down and begins to fall. If the plane happens to dive at the same time, it can be struck down by its own shell!

---

5.   Dr. Gina Cerminara, a famous author of Virginia Beach, Virginia, is a good friend of animals. Her motto is, "Those who can speak must speak for the wordless ones." She lectures on behalf of animals and exposes much of the cruelty and abuse toward them. Dr. Cerminara believes that cultivating love for all creatures helps us develop compassion and responsibility, and improves human personality.

1. The paragraph tells mainly—

    (A) what the silk fair of Baghdad was

    (B) what country Baghdad is in

    (C) why a cat is called a "tabby"

    (D) how all cats and fabrics are alike

2. The paragraph tells mainly—

    (A) who won a famous race

    (B) why contests are held

    (C) why people like to live in Lunenberg, Nova Scotia

    (D) how Lunenberg reflects its seafaring tradition

3. The paragraph tells mainly—

    (A) what silent sounds are

    (B) why people can't hear

    (C) how sound helps us

    (D) why ultrasonics are important

4. The paragraph tells mainly—

    (A) when jet airplane accidents occur

    (B) how jets crash

    (C) why jets never dive

    (D) how jets can shoot themselves

5. The paragraph tells mainly—

    (A) how well known Dr. Cerminara is as an author

    (B) what the motto of Dr. Cerminara is

    (C) where Dr. Cerminara lectures on animals

    (D) how Dr. Cerminara has worked on behalf of cats

1. What do you think is the most popular soda flavor in the United States? If you thought of cola, you are right. Almost two out of every three cans or bottles of soda that are sold are cola. The second most popular flavor is lemon-lime, but that is far behind cola. Orange, ginger ale, grape, and root beer are next down the list.

2. Electric companies may put a special "clock" in everyone's kitchen soon. Numbers flash on the screen of this "clock," telling how much electricity is being used in the home at the moment and how much the monthly electric bill is to that moment. Electric companies think people will use less electricity if they realize how much it is costing them.

3. Art in its many forms has built a bridge between our civilization and the cultures that preceded it. Pictures on pottery have revealed many aspects of the life and times of people of particular eras. The painter has pictured civilizations that once flourished and died. Music and dancing also reflect the characters and emotions of our ancestors.

4. Among those who guard the city of Philadelphia are thirty-five chickens. The birds are kept by Philadelphia's Health Department to help assure that no deadly disease strikes the city. Each summer the birds are allowed to be bitten by mosquitoes that fly around the city. The medical workers test the chickens' blood. If the blood contains no disease germs, doctors know the mosquitoes are harmless.

5. A buffalo stampede was a frightening thing to see. The shaggy-headed buffalo, each weighing from one to two thousand pounds, rushed forward, heads low, smashing, trampling, and destroying everything in their way. Their sharp hoofs kicked up dust as they rushed blindly forward, bringing death and destruction to anyone and anything unlucky enough to be caught in their path.

UNIT 12

1. The paragraph tells mainly—

   (A) how far behind cola lemon-lime is
   (B) why Americans prefer cola
   (C) what soda flavors Americans prefer
   (D) which nation drinks the most soda

2. The paragraph tells mainly—

   (A) when the special "clock" will operate
   (B) where the special "clock" will be
   (C) whom the special "clock" will be for
   (D) what the special "clock" will do

3. The paragraph tells mainly—

   (A) why artists like history
   (B) how music and dancing reveal the past
   (C) how people learn about themselves
   (D) how various art forms help people learn history

4. The paragraph tells mainly—

   (A) how birds protect a city
   (B) how mosquitoes infect birds
   (C) how mosquitoes carry diseases
   (D) how the Health Department thought of using chickens

5. The paragraph tells mainly—

   (A) how heavy buffalo are
   (B) what a buffalo stampede was like
   (C) how hard buffalo charge
   (D) why people are afraid of some animals

A. Exercising Your Skill

In Unit 8 you read about ancient coins. Do you know when coins were first used as money? Write down the century when you think they were first used, and then read the paragraph. _____

> Before coins as money came into common use, people bartered, or traded, goods for services or products. Animal hides, food, and gold and silver were once common articles of barter. Then someone invented money as an easier way to buy something. One theory says that the first coins appeared about 600 B.C. in what is now Turkey. A second theory says the Chinese used bronze coins years before that—perhaps as early as 1100 B.C. Whatever the earliest coins were, and whenever they were first issued, they are remarkably similar to modern coins. Both were designed by governments, and both have a value stamped on them.

Write the main idea of the paragraph. _____

B. Expanding Your Skill

As you read the next paragraph, look for the sentence that best states the main idea. It will be the one that sums up what the paragraph is mainly about.

> In the early days of America, tobacco was used as money, but so many people grew tobacco that it became worthless as a means of exchange. Throughout history many unusual objects have been used as money. Roman soldiers once received part of their pay in salt, which is the origin of our word *salary*, or payment for one's work. Early Egyptians used grains of wheat and corn as money, while natives on the island of Fiji used whale's teeth. Perhaps the most common object used as money was the seashell. Seashells were used in parts of Africa, and American Indians of long ago were using them as money, or *wampum*, as they called it, well before Columbus came to the New World.

Write the main idea sentence from the paragraph. _____

_____

Now write a title that sums up the main idea sentence. _____

_____

C. Exploring Language

Choose one of these main idea sentences and expand it into a paragraph of five or six sentences. Try to make your sentences support, or tell more about, the main idea sentence.

1. Money is a part of everybody's life.
2. Most people's main source of money is their salary—that is, what they are paid for the work they do.
3. Not everyone works for money.
4. The United States should issue paper money honoring a woman.
5. Few people stop to think about what money really is.

D. Expressing Yourself

Choose one of these activities.

1. Think of a few ways you spend money—for food, clothes, books, records, or whatever—each day. Then try to imagine a world without money. In a paragraph or two, describe what you would use as barter to get the products you wanted.

2. Design a new silver dollar coin. Decide whom, or what, you want to honor. Then make a drawing of your design, both front and back sides. Make your drawing at least six inches across so every detail of your coin will show clearly. Give your coin a name: "The _____ Silver Dollar."

3. Make believe that you have just won a lottery for one million dollars. Write a paragraph describing what you would do with the money. Would you spend it all? Would you save it all? Would you share it with anyone else?

4. Have a debate with one of your classmates. Each of you choose one of the following sides: *The love of money is the root of all evil*; *The love of money is not the root of all evil.*

1.   Probably the most unusual school anywhere was the Holloman Air Force Aeromedical Research Laboratory in New Mexico, where classes were conducted for forty chimpanzees who would be making space flights. The astrochimps' training included plane and rocket-sled rides to familiarize them with weightlessness. They also underwent isolation training and mental exercises. Chimps were selected for this school on the basis of their intelligence, age, personality, and physical characteristics.

2.   That car parked in front of your home has come from all over the world. Countries from Australia to Zambia ship materials to U.S. car makers. Different metals come from all five continents. Some small parts are made of cork from Spain. Jute and cotton for cushions and padding come from Japan and Egypt. Rubber for tires is taken from trees in faraway Southeast Asia.

3.   The lowest and hottest spot in the United States is in Death Valley. This valley, located in California near the Nevada border, is 282 feet below sea level. Temperatures of 125 degrees Fahrenheit (52 Celsius) are common. In 1931 a temperature of 134 degrees F. (56.7 C.) was noted, a record high for the nation. A group of gold seekers gave the valley its grim name in 1849.

4.   What are the tallest plants in the world? Many people would say the giant redwood trees of California. Actually, the tallest plants are in the oceans. These are seaweeds that grow almost seven hundred feet tall. Compared to this height, the giant redwoods are pygmies of only four hundred feet. To get some idea of these heights, consider the Statue of Liberty. This huge figure rises only three hundred feet.

5.   About the year 1516 there appeared a coin known as a Joachimsthaler. The silver in the coin was mined in Joachim's Dale, a mining area in central Europe. The coin became popular all over Europe, and the name was shortened to thaler. The English found *thaler* rather difficult to say and used *dollar* in its place. This is the word we use today.

1. The paragraph tells mainly—

    (A) who trained the astrochimps for flight
    (B) where the Air Force trained chimpanzees
    (C) how chimpanzees were selected for training
    (D) what made one school in New Mexico so unusual

2. The paragraph tells mainly—

    (A) who decides where car parts will be bought
    (B) how parts of cars are shipped here
    (C) why rubber must come from Southeast Asia
    (D) where parts of cars come from

3. The paragraph tells mainly—

    (A) how Death Valley got its name
    (B) where Death Valley is located
    (C) why it gets warm in California
    (D) what Death Valley is like

4. The paragraph tells mainly—

    (A) where the Statue of Liberty stands
    (B) where redwoods are found
    (C) why seaweed grows
    (D) what the tallest plants are

5. The paragraph tells mainly—

    (A) where money comes from
    (B) how the word *dollar* originated
    (C) how people make dollars
    (D) why the English found *thaler* difficult to say

UNIT 14

1.   Unlike most other spiders, the wolf spider spins no web. Instead it lives in a small hole in the ground. It lines this hole with silken material like that with which other spiders spin their webs. Then the wolf spider makes a lid for its hole. The little creature even spins a silken hinge for the snug-fitting lid. Inside its burrow, this spider is safe from all enemies.

2.   What causes the beautiful blue haze that blankets the Smoky Mountains of Tennessee and North Carolina? One professor says that the "blue smoke" of these mountains is really caused by the pine trees, which give off hydrocarbons. The hydrocarbons react to sunlight and form other substances. These substances mix with water droplets to create the little particles of matter that make the "smoke" in the atmosphere.

3.   The world's biggest sporting event is not the World Series or the Super Bowl, nor even the Olympics. It is the World Cup soccer contest. Soccer is the national sport of more countries than any other sport. So sixteen top national teams from around the world play every four years to see which is the world's champion. Crowds of over 100,000 cheer each game for the World Cup.

4.   During the early 1900s, one-third of all the automobiles in America were powered by electric batteries. The oldest remaining model is on exhibit at the Smithsonian Institution in Washington, D.C. It resembles a stagecoach. The driver sat behind the body on a raised seat over the battery compartment—peeking out at the road over the roof and steering with a tiller, a kind of handle used to steer a boat.

5.   There is little truth to most of the stories told about vampire bats, yet the most fantastic story is true. This ugly creature does drink blood. It settles on a sleeping victim. When it finds an exposed spot, it slashes the skin with its razor-sharp teeth. The blood starts to ooze out, and the vampire has its nightly fill.

UNIT 14

1. The paragraph tells mainly—

   (A) why the wolf spider spins no web
   (B) how the wolf spider builds its home
   (C) how the wolf spider spins its web
   (D) why the wolf spider lives in the ground

2. The paragraph tells mainly—

   (A) why people like the Smoky Mountains
   (B) how smoky the mountains get
   (C) what causes the Smokies to be smoky
   (D) why people smoke

3. The paragraph tells mainly—

   (A) why so many countries like soccer
   (B) what the biggest sporting event is
   (C) how many teams play for the World Cup
   (D) where the World Cup games are played

4. The paragraph tells mainly—

   (A) how automobiles used to be powered
   (B) when electric automobiles were popular in America
   (C) what the old-fashioned electric car was like
   (D) why electric automobiles were used

5. The paragraph tells mainly—

   (A) why vampire bats work only at night
   (B) why there is little truth to some stories
   (C) why the vampire bat drinks blood
   (D) what the vampire bat does

1.   The wolf's blood-curdling howl is generally thought to signal danger to anyone nearby. A Canadian researcher has discovered that this is often far from true. Wolves frequently like to get together and howl just for fun. After a pack of wolves finish howling, they bark happily and wag their tails. Wolves also use their howls to identify each other. They can recognize wolves of their own or another pack.

2.   What has been the greatest of all inventions? Most experts agree that it is the wheel. Imagine what life would be like without cars, trains, or even wagons! Some unknown person in the Middle East first thought of wheels, probably about six thousand years ago. We know this from ancient drawings. Once humans had the use of wheels, they could pull far greater loads and travel much farther.

3.   The name *scrod* was coined by a Boston restaurant. It means a small size fish of any edible kind. This restaurant had a reputation for serving only the freshest fish. But who knows what will be the freshest catch of the boats unloading at fish markets at 5 A.M. on any given day? By calling all such fish *scrod*, the Boston restaurant could serve "fresh scrod" daily.

4.   On the island of Gomera, one of the Canary Islands, people communicate with each other in a strange way. This island off the coast of Africa is extremely mountainous. Its people, therefore, have for years communicated with each other across deep ravines by whistling from the hills. The shrill, whistling notes carry clearly for several miles.

5.   In the 1700s, King George III of England founded a peculiar holiday—Bean Day! While inspecting the construction of a military establishment near London, he smelled something cooking. It was baked beans and bacon. Never having heard of the dish before, the king sat down and ate lunch with his workers. Because he so enjoyed this feast with his subjects, the king instituted a yearly bean celebration.

1. The paragraph tells mainly—

   (A) where wolves howl
   (B) how wolves howl
   (C) why wolves howl
   (D) who discovered wolves' howls

2. The paragraph tells mainly—

   (A) how life would be without wheels
   (B) when the wheel was invented
   (C) what the greatest invention is
   (D) who invented the wheel

3. The paragraph tells mainly—

   (A) what the letters of the word *scrod* stand for
   (B) what the word *scrod* means today
   (C) why the word *scrod* was invented
   (D) when scrod is served in restaurants

4. The paragraph tells mainly—

   (A) why people often whistle
   (B) how people signal one another
   (C) how the people of Gomera communicate
   (D) how far the whistled notes carry

5. The paragraph tells mainly—

   (A) where King George III established Bean Day
   (B) how England's yearly Bean Day started
   (C) why baked beans were served to the king
   (D) why King George III of England ate with commoners

UNIT 16

1.   In 1859 an Australian rancher freed two dozen European wild rabbits from the family ranch. In less than a hundred years the rabbit population of Australia jumped to about 500 million. Swarms of rabbits were devouring pasture grasses needed by sheep. A virus introduced into the rabbit population killed 400 million of them. Scientists are looking for new ways to kill most of the remaining 100 million rabbits.

2.   Can an earthworm learn from experience? An experiment was conducted. Every time a worm turned right it was shocked with a jolt of electricity. After hundreds of efforts, the earthworm slowly learned to turn to the left. Furthermore, even when its head was cut off, the earthworm "remembered" the lesson. It simply grew a new head and continued to turn in the correct direction!

3.   Police in many cities have found a good way to patrol downtown areas. They use bicycles. Police officers pedal around on ten-speed bikes. They can ride up to any situation much easier than if they were in a car. They can stop trouble before it starts. Police on bicycles make people feel safer.

4.   Native American women made excellent guides for travelers in the new America. They often knew several languages and had skills to help the explorers find food. They knew how to treat illnesses and mend broken bones. They could also repair the birchbark canoes used for traveling. European explorers would, literally, have been lost without their Native American guides.

5.   The turkeylike maleos are famous for their clever ways of hatching their eggs. At breeding time, many maleos head for shore lands to deposit their eggs in holes dug in black sand. This dark sand has a greater capacity to store heat. Other maleos bury their eggs in soil near hot springs or in earth heated by volcanic steam.

1. The paragraph tells mainly—

   (A) what burrows the rabbits of Australia are building
   (B) how the rabbit population of Australia has changed
   (C) why Australia needs more rabbits
   (D) what the virus did to the rabbits

2. The paragraph tells mainly—

   (A) how earthworms remember
   (B) why earthworms forget
   (C) what earthworms do
   (D) what one earthworm learned

3. The paragraph tells mainly—

   (A) where to find police on bicycles
   (B) how police on bicycles dress
   (C) what kind of bicycles the police use
   (D) how police on bicycles help prevent trouble

4. The paragraph tells mainly—

   (A) how European explorers got lost
   (B) how many languages Native American women spoke
   (C) how birchbark canoes often were damaged
   (D) how skilled Native American women served as guides

5. The paragraph tells mainly—

   (A) how maleos behave
   (B) how maleos hatch their eggs
   (C) why maleos prefer dark sand
   (D) how hot springs help maleos

1.   Texas longhorns were not like the gentle, fat, slow-moving cattle of today. They were huge—weighing over a thousand pounds—and were almost as fast as deer. They had a fighting spirit, pointed horns that they enjoyed tossing, sharp hooves, and a deep dislike for anything in their way. The Texas longhorns were fierce animals that commanded respect from people—and even from grizzly bears!

---

2.   Few people are aware of the huge size of Canada. It is the second largest country in the world. Only Russia is larger. Canada reaches one-fourth of the way around the world. It has more lakes than the rest of the world's countries combined. Yet there are but 24 million people in this vast land, only about as many as in the state of California.

---

3.   The Haskell Opera House lies partly in the United States, partly in Canada. The entrance is in America, but the stage is in Canada. Local people tell about a man wanted by the American police. He was discovered performing on the stage of the Haskell Opera House. Since he stayed in the Canadian half of the building, and so was in a foreign country, American authorities couldn't arrest him!

---

4.   Canada is more than a land of great beauty. It is also a land of vast forests. Lumber and the products that come from lumber make Canada a leader in world paper production. The pulp and paper industry continues to grow and is now Canada's leading industry.

---

5.   Communication means a sharing of information. People communicate with each other in many ways. Much communication is face-to-face and silent. People smile and laugh. They shake hands. They wave. They squeeze a friend's hand to communicate sympathy or greetings. People share information about how they feel, often without as much as a single word.

1. The paragraph tells mainly—

    (A) how big the Texas longhorns were
    (B) what Texas longhorns were like
    (C) why grizzly bears ran away
    (D) what the horns of the Texas longhorns were like

2. The paragraph tells mainly—

    (A) where Canada is located
    (B) why few people live in Canada
    (C) how large Canada is
    (D) how many lakes Canada has

3. The paragraph tells mainly—

    (A) where the Haskell Opera House is located
    (B) why the police wanted to arrest a performer
    (C) what strange event occurred at the Haskell Opera House
    (D) which part of the Haskell Opera House is in America

4. The paragraph tells mainly—

    (A) how many trees there are
    (B) why Canada has so many trees
    (C) what Canada gets from its forests
    (D) why Canada is so beautiful

5. The paragraph tells mainly—

    (A) what information means
    (B) how people communicate without words
    (C) how people show sympathy by squeezing hands
    (D) why words aren't important

1. Ranchers like to find locoweed. It is a sign that something worth much money is under the ground. This plant, which poisons horses and cattle, grows above deposits of selenium. The selenium comes from uranium ore, which is very valuable in the atomic energy field. Thus the locoweed is a sign of treasure worth more than gold.

2. An instrument has been invented for finding diamonds. The device directs X-rays over gravel that has been taken from diamond mines. The radiation causes any diamonds in the gravel to twinkle. The twinkling causes a blast of air, which blows the diamond off the sorting table and into a container.

3. Did you ever dream that your bicycle could fly? Well, over a hundred years ago an American inventor made one that really could. A professor hung a seat and a set of pedals beneath a ten-foot-long balloon. The professor's pedaling turned a propeller. This balloon bicycle really flew—for an hour. Then the professor's legs got tired, and the flying bike had to land.

4. More than half the produce of Canada's fisheries comes from the waters off the Atlantic Provinces—Newfoundland, New Brunswick, Nova Scotia, and Prince Edward Island. Lobster, cod, halibut, sardines, clams, herring, and mackerel are the leading varieties. With a yearly Atlantic catch worth well over $60 million, fishers from these provinces place Canada high on the list of fish-producing countries.

5. Hunters know that all Labrador retrievers make good hunting dogs. However, it is doubtful that any other Labrador is as skilled as "Duke, the duck-calling dog." Duke has been trained to call ducks with a duck call. When they approach, Duke fires a stationary shotgun. Then, if any ducks have been hit, the dog swims out and retrieves them. Duke now displays his talents at sports shows.

1. The paragraph tells mainly—
    - (A) how valuable uranium ore is
    - (B) what locoweed looks like
    - (C) why ranchers like to find locoweed
    - (D) why cattle like to eat locoweed

2. The paragraph tells mainly—
    - (A) why diamonds must be valuable to people
    - (B) how an invention helps to identify diamonds
    - (C) how diamonds are mined
    - (D) why diamonds twinkle

3. The paragraph tells mainly—
    - (A) who invented the flying bicycle
    - (B) when the flying bicycle was invented
    - (C) what the flying bicycle was like
    - (D) why the flying bicycle had to land

4. The paragraph tells mainly—
    - (A) how the Atlantic fisheries are important to Canada
    - (B) why Canadians like to fish
    - (C) how many lobsters Nova Scotians catch each year
    - (D) where the Atlantic Provinces are

5. The paragraph tells mainly—
    - (A) why Labradors like hunting
    - (B) where Labradors hunt
    - (C) what one Labrador can do
    - (D) how Labradors retrieve ducks

1.   On June 11, 1897, a group of explorers attempted to fly over the North Pole in a balloon. Thirty-three years later, other explorers discovered the frozen bodies of the balloonists, undeveloped film, and a journal. From this evidence they learned that the balloon had been forced down. After journeying toward civilization for two and a half months, the balloon explorers had died of starvation and cold.

2.   Among early New England families there was little difference between the food served at breakfast and that served at dinner. Often breakfast was the larger meal. Sturdy New England breakfast tables groaned under mounds of potatoes, great juicy steaks, mushrooms, wheatcakes, fruit, and tangy maple syrup. No breakfast was complete without pie. How times have changed!

3.   Is nature more efficient than machinery? Farming records show that in some cases it is not. Corn uses sunshine better than other plants, but it wastes about ninety-nine percent of the sunlight that reaches it. If plants were as efficient as machinery, the results would be startling. It would be possible to raise three tons of corn on a single acre in just one day!

4.   When telling a lie, a person breathes a little more rapidly than usual. The heart beats faster and the blood pressure rises. A person can't control these changes. They always occur when a lie is told. Police have a device to measure these changes when they question suspects. It is known as a lie detector, or polygraph.

5.   How do we release the sound that is "frozen" into an LP record? The needle on the pickup head travels through the grooves as the record turns. The zigzag lines in the grooves make the needle vibrate. These vibrations of the needle are changed into vibrations of an electric current. The vibrations of the electric current are strengthened and changed into sound.

1. The paragraph tells mainly—

    (A) how many attempted this flight
    (B) why the balloon was forced down
    (C) how the expedition's fate was learned
    (D) who discovered the North Pole

2. The paragraph tells mainly—

    (A) why early New Englanders liked pie
    (B) why breakfast was such an important meal in New England
    (C) what breakfast was like in early New England
    (D) why tables had to be sturdy

3. The paragraph tells mainly—

    (A) what farming records show
    (B) when corn grows
    (C) which plant uses sunshine best
    (D) how plants and machines compare

4. The paragraph tells mainly—

    (A) why some people sometimes tell lies
    (B) how to raise your blood pressure
    (C) what happens when people lie
    (D) how the lie detector was invented

5. The paragraph tells mainly—

    (A) how we get sound from records
    (B) why vibrations are bad for stereo needles
    (C) who makes records
    (D) what the word *record* means

A. Exercising Your Skill

Everyone has a name. In the following paragraph, you will read about some unusual names of people.

A surprising number of people have last names that are unusual because they fit the job the person has. For example, there is the man named Rockett who works for NASA. Then there is a dentist named Toothman, a man named James Rotton who studies the effects of pollution, and Paul Hammer, who works in a machine shop. Continuing, you can find a geologist whose name is Donald Stone, a lawyer named Hugh Law, and a man named Jack J. Barber, who is, yes, a barber. Finally, there really is a family named Gunn whose daughter, Betty B., goes by her initials, while her brother Thomas likes to be called "Tommy." As for Mr. Gunn, his name is Richard, but, as you may have guessed, everyone calls him "Pop"!

Write the main idea sentence. _____

B. Expanding Your Skill

Every paragraph has a main idea, but sometimes that idea is unstated. Every paragraph also has supporting sentences. They tell more about the main idea, even when it is not directly stated. Read the paragraph below.

History, as many people have noted, was reversed in 1979 when President Jimmy Carter cleared Dr. Samuel Mudd of any blame in the 1865 assassination of President Abraham Lincoln. It was Dr. Mudd who tended the broken leg of assassin John Wilkes Booth. Dr. Mudd went to prison for four years, although he did not know that Booth had shot Lincoln until after he had helped the man. For 114 years generations of Mudds had petitioned presidents to clear the name of their ancestor. Finally, President Carter did just that. As one TV reporter noted at the time, the sting was removed from the old saying "His name is mud."

Write the main idea, and tell if it is stated or unstated.

_____

Write two details that support the main idea. _____

_____

C. Exploring Language

Choose one of these main-idea sentences and expand it into a paragraph of five or six sentences. Try to make most of the sentences you write support the main-idea sentence.

1. I would like to change my name.
2. People should be allowed to pick their own first name when they are old enough to read.
3. Names play an important role in how some people feel about themselves.
4. My favorite name is _____ because _____ .
5. Children should be named after their grandfathers or grandmothers.

D. Expressing Yourself

Choose one of these activities.

1. Explain the meaning of each of these terms. Then give an example if you can.
   a. family name
   b. given name
   c. legal name
   d. nickname
   e. pen name
   f. pseudonym
   g. stage name
   h. surname

2. Nearly every name has a meaning. For example, Barbara means "stranger," and Margaret means "pearl." Eric means "kingly," and Robert means "bright fame." See if you can find out what your first name or middle name means, then write a short paragraph explaining what it means.

3. Make up a list of unusual names that fit a person's job, such as Dr. Toothman, the dentist. See if you can invent ten such names.

4. Pretend that you have ten children—five boys and five girls. Write down the names that you gave your children. Give each child a first and middle name.

UNIT 20

1. The human body can adapt itself remarkably to difficult conditions of living. For example, people who live high in the Andes Mountains, where the air is very thin, have an extra quart of blood in their bodies to help them get enough oxygen. Also, from years of walking barefoot in the cold, these people have grown extra blood vessels in their feet. They can walk barefoot even in snow without discomfort.

2. We think of the collie, German shepherd, Great Dane, Newfoundland, and Saint Bernard as fun-loving pets. Once these famous breeds were just work dogs with special duties to perform. The collie and German shepherd were flock tenders. The Great Dane was a property guard. The Newfoundland was the world's champion lifesaver. The Saint Bernard broke trails for people over deep snowfalls in the Alps mountains.

3. Perhaps the world's most violent snowstorm is the purga. This dreaded blizzard sweeps over northern Siberia in winter. Its violence is so great that people cannot open their eyes. Many people even report difficulty in standing upright. People caught in this blinding storm often become lost and freeze to death within yards of the doorways to their homes.

4. Ancient papyrus sheets have been discovered in the sands of Egypt. They have been preserved by the dryness of the climate. One sheet contains a laundry list: "fine tunics 2, dalmatics 2, breeches 2, felt slippers 1, carpetbag, ground-sheet, small pillow, etc." A letter sent home by a school child ends with a postscript, "Please feed my pigeons." How like our own were the daily lives of these people!

5. There is a worm in the sea that is actually a living fishline! This is the fishline worm. It can be found curled up under a rock. It looks small, but when it uncoils it is eighty feet long. The sharp teeth of the worm attach themselves to a small fish. Once they do, they never let go. Finally the fish tires of fighting the long worm. The fishline worm then devours its catch.

1.   The paragraph tells mainly—

    (A) how Andean people get cold from walking barefoot

    (B) what the air is like in the Andes

    (C) how people's bodies can adjust to a climate

    (D) how much oxygen everyone's blood needs

2.   The paragraph tells mainly—

    (A) which dogs are fun-loving pets

    (B) where some dogs were used to guard property

    (C) why some dogs were used to do work

    (D) how certain pet dogs were once work animals

3.   The paragraph tells mainly—

    (A) how often the purga occurs

    (B) what happens in winter

    (C) why people can't open their eyes

    (D) why the purga is dreaded

4.   The paragraph tells mainly—

    (A) where papyrus sheets were discovered

    (B) how the papyrus sheets were preserved

    (C) what one school child of ancient Egypt wrote

    (D) what the papyrus sheets reveal

5.   The paragraph tells mainly—

    (A) how the worm uncoils

    (B) what kinds of fish are caught

    (C) how fishline worms are caught

    (D) how a worm catches fish

UNIT 21

1. Gold is soft—almost as soft as putty. It can be hammered into a thin wafer five millionths of an inch thick without being heated. Just one ounce of gold can be beaten into a thin sheet a hundred feet square, or drawn into a thin wire stretching fifty miles. In addition, gold is a superb conductor of electricity and a marvelous reflector of heat and light.

2. An invention known as the flashing phone helps the deaf. A device is connected to a telephone, and the deaf person can "see" the phone messages in flashes of light, or "feel" the messages in the vibrations of a finger pad. By using the sensing key on the unit, the deaf person can send light or vibration signals to others who possess a set.

3. Maine's rocky coast and forest-covered mountains make it the summer playground of the East. Sports-lovers are attracted to the state for hunting and fishing. Bathers enjoy its sandy beaches and sparkling lakes. Few visitors, whether sports enthusiasts or sightseers, can resist trying Maine's delicious boiled lobsters. None can ignore the splendor of Maine's scenery.

4. A slow and gradual movement of earth downhill is called "creep." It occurs so slowly that it is sometimes not noticed. It results in tilted telephone poles and fences, and cracked walls and sidewalks. Creep can be caused by the forces of gravity pulling upon the top layers of a gentle slope. Changes in temperature resulting in contraction and expansion can also cause creep.

5. Some animals such as the cheetah have blazing speed. The cheetah can run at speeds as high as eighty miles an hour. The animal kingdom has its slowpokes too. The porcupine is among the slowest. Because of its quills, it does not need to escape enemies. It can lumber along in peace at two miles an hour. Slowest of all is the sloth. It moves at a speed of just one mile per hour!

UNIT 21

1. The paragraph tells mainly—
   (A) why gold reflects heat and light
   (B) why gold is so soft
   (C) what makes metals so valuable
   (D) what wonderful qualities gold has

2. The paragraph tells mainly—
   (A) how inventions help people
   (B) how the deaf learn
   (C) how people get vibrations
   (D) how the flashing phone helps the deaf

3. The paragraph tells mainly—
   (A) why Maine is full of trees
   (B) why swimmers enjoy Maine
   (C) what people eat in Maine
   (D) what Maine offers

4. The paragraph tells mainly—
   (A) what creep is
   (B) why poles crack and fences tilt
   (C) what gravity is
   (D) what gravity does

5. The paragraph tells mainly—
   (A) how speeds of animals differ
   (B) how fast the cheetah is
   (C) why the porcupine is slow
   (D) what animal is the slowest of all

1.   The insect called *Halobates*, or water strider, lives its entire life in the middle of the ocean, without ever touching land. It can "run" rapidly across the surface of the water. Using four of its six legs to balance itself on the water's surface, it can grab and hold food with the other two. It even lays its eggs on floating objects.

2.   The people of China have an old saying that rings true. They say, "A journey of a thousand miles begins with one step." By this they mean that when starting something new or undertaking a project, it is often the first action that is the most difficult. Yet it is this first step that is necessary before the second and third and following steps can be taken.

3.   Fairs have been held since ancient times. As long as three thousand years ago, the Chinese held fairs. During the Middle Ages great fairs displayed fine products and were held all over Europe. People everywhere in all eras have loved fairs—and still do. For centuries people have flocked to fairs to admire and to buy, just as they do today.

4.   Newspapers in the Old West often had colorful names. Some of the more interesting were *Kicker, Avalanche, Burro,* and *The Solid Muldoon.* What were these papers like? It is hard to say. Most frontier journals rushed on and off the scene faster than a tumbleweed in a dust storm, leaving little trace of their passing, other than their unique names.

5.   The American cavalry defeated and conquered every American Indian tribe except one. The Seminole Indians of Florida couldn't and wouldn't be beaten. Under the leadership of their chief, Osceola, the Seminoles won one battle after another against the cavalry. Some forty thousand American soldiers were put into the field against about fifteen thousand Seminole braves. Nothing could make the Seminoles surrender, and they remained unconquered.

1. The paragraph tells mainly—

    (A) what *Halobates* looks like
    (B) how many legs *Halobates* has
    (C) how *Halobates* lives on water
    (D) what *Halobates* lays eggs on

2. The paragraph tells mainly—

    (A) why the Chinese make sure to tell the truth
    (B) how to take one big step
    (C) what an old Chinese expression means
    (D) why some things are difficult

3. The paragraph tells mainly—

    (A) why Chinese hold fairs
    (B) why people like to buy things
    (C) how fairs have been held through the ages
    (D) what products people buy at fairs

4. The paragraph tells mainly—

    (A) what the Old West was like
    (B) who published newspapers
    (C) why newspapers go out of business
    (D) what interesting names frontier newspapers had

5. The paragraph tells mainly—

    (A) where the Seminole Indians lived
    (B) which American Indian tribe remained unconquered
    (C) how many battles the Seminoles won against the cavalry
    (D) which Indian tribe elected Osceola as its chief

1. Steel-mill workers used to be among the world's most uncomfortable people. They work near furnaces in temperatures up to 140 degrees Fahrenheit (60 Celsius). The furnaces give off so much heat that the mills cannot be air-conditioned. An ice-vest was invented to keep workers cool. Blocks of dry ice fit into the vest and cool the worker who wears it.

2. Long before modern people sent messages by telegraph, the ancient Greeks had a telegraph of their own. Unlike the modern version, with its tapping code and its use of electricity, the Greeks had a torch telegraph. It consisted of frames and iron rings on hilltops. Torches were placed in certain rings that corresponded to the Greek alphabet. The torches were arranged and rearranged to spell the desired message.

3. The owl and the crow prey on each other's weaknesses. At night, owls often make dinners of crows, which cannot see well in the dark. During the day it's a different story. Vengeful groups of crows attack and kill sleeping owls, which are resting for another night of hunting!

4. Identifying rocks is not easy. With practice, however, it becomes easy to recognize common types. The color of a rock is not a very reliable clue to its identity, but hardness is a good identification test. Another test is luster. There are many books that contain aids for identifying one's "finds," as well as other very useful information.

5. The first telephone directory in the world was issued in New Haven, Connecticut, in 1878. It was a simple card listing fifty subscribers, among them a minister and ten leading business people and officials. Also listed were three doctors, two dentists, twenty stores and factories, four meat and fish markets, two workhorse stables, a post office, drugstore, police station, two men's clubs, and the *Yale News*.

1. The paragraph tells mainly—

    (A) who invented the ice-vest
    (B) why steel mills are so hot
    (C) how steel-mill workers can be cooled
    (D) where the world's most uncomfortable people are

2. The paragraph tells mainly—

    (A) how the modern telegraph works
    (B) how torches were placed in certain rings
    (C) how torches sent messages in ancient Greece
    (D) how rings had to correspond with the Greek alphabet

3. The paragraph tells mainly—

    (A) what owls do at night
    (B) what crows eat
    (C) how birds fight
    (D) what owls and crows do to each other

4. The paragraph tells mainly—

    (A) how to give tests
    (B) how books help rock collectors
    (C) how to identify rocks
    (D) why people collect rocks

5. The paragraph tells mainly—

    (A) when the first telephone directory was issued
    (B) what the first telephone directory contained
    (C) why the first telephone directory was issued
    (D) where the first telephone directory was issued

1.   We think of a flood or an earthquake as a natural disaster. To many of nature's animals, however, the greatest disaster is the coming of large numbers of humans. When settlers came from the East to America's great western plains, they killed millions of bison, poisoned the prairie dogs, and shot the coyotes. All this upset the area's balance of nature. For the animals, it was worse than a flood or an earthquake.

---

2.   The king cobra of Asia has the worst reputation of any poisonous snake. This reptile reaches a length of almost twenty feet and has an extremely powerful venom. A single bite from the "King of Poison" proves fatal within three or four hours. In some instances death occurs within an hour. Each year almost ten thousand people are killed by cobras.

---

3.   About three hundred Native Americans live in the Grand Canyon of Arizona. The Havasupai, or "people of the blue water," have their own town, called Supai, on the canyon floor. The only way to visit is by helicopter or on horseback down a long, winding, frightening trail. The Havasupai grow their own food and cook over outdoor fires. For recreation, they swim in the nearby river and have rodeos.

---

4.   Long ago, French soldiers stationed in Canada were without money. A government official took all the playing cards the soldiers had, made each part of a card worth a sum of money, and signed each one. The soldiers used the cards for money. No one refused to accept the card money. Years later, people with card money were paid back in real money.

---

5.   People who live in the country have mail delivered to them, just as do villagers and city-dwellers. Their service is called R.F.D., meaning Rural Free Delivery. *Rural* means "country." The R.F.D. worker picks up mail and delivers it to the family box, which is situated on top of a roadside post in front of each home.

1.   The paragraph tells mainly—

   (A) how nature balances itself
   (B) how many animals the settlers killed
   (C) how floods and earthquakes affect animals
   (D) how humans can be a disaster to nature

2.   The paragraph tells mainly—

   (A) where the king cobra snake lives
   (B) how poisonous the king cobra is
   (C) how many people die
   (D) how long the king cobra is

3.   The paragraph tells mainly—

   (A) where and how the Havasupai Indians live
   (B) what the Havasupai call their town
   (C) how to visit the Havasupai Indians
   (D) where the Havasupai cook their food

4.   The paragraph tells mainly—

   (A) who used playing-card money
   (B) how French Canadians gambled
   (C) how French soldiers lived
   (D) how playing-card money originated

5.   The paragraph tells mainly—

   (A) how R.F.D. started
   (B) where the family mailbox is
   (C) what R.F.D. is
   (D) what *rural* means

1.   If you think the ostrich is a big bird, you should have seen the moa bird. There are no more moas alive today, though they existed until only a few hundred years before Columbus. A moa looked something like a thick-legged ostrich, but it was twelve feet high—over twice as tall as most humans. The tiny kiwi bird is a surviving cousin of the moa.

___

2.   How remarkable our bodies are! In twelve hours the human heart uses enough energy to lift a fifty-six-ton railroad car one foot off the earth! Someone weighing 140 pounds contains enough fat to make seven cakes of soap, carbon for 9,000 pencils, phosphorus for 2,200 match heads, iron for one nail, lime to whitewash a chicken coop, sulfur to remove a dog's fleas, and water to fill a ten-gallon barrel!

___

3.   Some "modern" inventions are much older than we may think. Telephones and electric lights are over a century old. Washing machines, elevators, and ice-making machines were invented in the 1850s. Bicycles and steam shovels date from the 1830s. In 1822 electric motors were invented. Submarines, tractors, and steam engines go back to the 1700s, and adding machines to the 1600s.

___

4.   Of all the stories about the loyalty of dogs, the one about Greyfriar's Bobby, a Skye terrier, is the most amazing. When Bobby's master died, the stout-hearted little dog attended the funeral. After all the mourners had left, Bobby stayed on. For the remaining fourteen years of his life, Bobby stood watch over his master's grave!

___

5.   The ice-cream cone was born at the St. Louis World's Fair in 1904. A person selling sugar waffles came to the rescue of an ice-cream vendor who had run out of dishes. The waffle-seller offered some waffles to use as a crude sort of "cone" to hold the ice cream. The ice-cream cone has been a best-seller ever since.

1. The paragraph tells mainly—

    (A) why the moa bird became extinct
    (B) when the moa bird became extinct
    (C) what the moa bird was like
    (D) what relative of the moa bird survived

2. The paragraph tells mainly—

    (A) what can be done with the phosphorus in the body
    (B) how remarkably strong the human heart is
    (C) why the makeup of a human being is astonishing
    (D) how much sulfur the human body contains

3. The paragraph tells mainly—

    (A) how several things work
    (B) who invented several things
    (C) why several things were invented
    (D) when several things were invented

4. The paragraph tells mainly—

    (A) what Greyfriar's Bobby did
    (B) how Bobby's master died
    (C) where Bobby lived
    (D) how long Bobby stood watch

5. The paragraph tells mainly—

    (A) why people like ice cream
    (B) how waffles help
    (C) how the ice-cream cone was born
    (D) what happened years ago

The Last L A P
Language Activity Pages

A. Exercising Your Skill

Nature includes many storms such as the purga described in Unit 20. One of the most harmful storms is the hurricane. Think what you already know about hurricanes. Then write four or five sentences in support of this main idea sentence.

> The hurricane is one of the most harmful storms. _____
> _____
> _____
> _____
> _____

Now read the following paragraph.

Australians call hurricanes "willy-willies." The Japanese know them as typhoons. We in North America refer to them as hurricanes. By whatever name, the hurricane is a killer storm. A storm becomes a hurricane when its winds exceed 72 miles per hour, but they have been known to reach well over 200 m.p.h.! Put this information together with the fact that the average hurricane measures 400 miles across, and you can perhaps begin to imagine how awesome a hurricane can be.

> Write the sentence that states the main idea of the paragraph.
> _____
> Now write a title that sums up the main idea.
> _____

B. Expanding Your Skill

Write two supporting sentences from the passage that helped you decide on the title you wrote.

Exchange papers with a classmate. He or she will write a third supporting sentence from the paragraph to go with the title you chose.

> 1. _____
> 2. _____

C. Exploring Language

Choose one of these activities.

1. Here are several sentences about hurricanes. Look for the main idea sentence and its supporting sentences. Then rearrange the supporting sentences into a clear paragraph. Do not include the two sentences that do not support the main idea sentence. Finally, give the paragraph a title.

- The eye of a hurricane is usually about 14 miles across.
- Winds stretch out from the eye several hundred miles in all directions.
- The shape of a hurricane is unique.
- The word "hurricane" comes from a West Indian word, *huracan*, which means "evil spirit."
- It is the only storm that has a calm center, or "eye."
- Winds and rains around the eye are the strongest.
- The hurricane season in the Northern Hemisphere lasts from June through November.
- However, an eye twice the normal size is not unusual.
- Air around the eye swirls upward like smoke in a chimney.

Write your title for the paragraph. _____

2. Write four or five sentences in support of the following main idea.

The real damage from a hurricane occurs when the storm strikes an area where a lot of people live.

D. Expressing Yourself

Choose one of these activities.

1. Go to the library and find out the name of one major hurricane that has hit the United States since 1900. Write a newspaper article describing the hurricane and its effects. Remember to include **Who**, **What**, **When**, **Where**, **Why**, and **How**.
2. Imagine what a hurricane at sea must look like. Draw a picture showing a sailing vessel being battered by a hurricane. Give it a title.
3. What are other natural disasters? Write two or three paragraphs about other natural disasters and how they are harmful.

63